The Instant
Meals in a Jar
Cookbook

The Instant Pot®
Meals in a Jar
Cookbook

50 PRE-PORTIONED, PERFECTLY SEASONED
PRESSURE COOKER RECIPES

PAMELA ELLGEN

 ULYSSES PRESS

Published by:
ULYSSES PRESS
P.O. Box 3440
Berkeley, CA 94703
www.ulyssespress.com

ISBN: 978-1-61243-894-8
Library of Congress Control Number: 2018967990

Printed in the United States by Versa Press
10 9 8 7 6 5 4 3

Acquisitions editor: Casie Vogel
Managing editor: Claire Chun
Editor: Renee Rutledge
Proofreader: Shayna Keyles
Front cover design: Hannah Rohrs
Interior design: what!design @ whatweb.com
Production: Jake Flaherty

Contents

Introduction

Welcome to *The Instant Pot® Meals in a Jar Cookbook*. In this book, you'll discover delicious recipes that fill your pantry with easy-to-make meals and provide awesome gifts for your friends and family. I am a busy working mom who longs to feed my family nutritious meals that are big on flavor but don't require hours in the kitchen. I also want to prepare thoughtful gifts for my friends and family for birthdays, holidays, or when they've had a new baby or another life change. Thanks to the Instant Pot pressure cooker and a few inexpensive mason jars, I can do both!

This book is laid out in a user-friendly format with recipes grouped according to the meal type and the type of ingredients.

In the Breakfast chapter, I offer recipes that you can toss into the Instant Pot when you wake up. Breakfast will be ready by the time you emerge from the shower.

In Snacks, Sides, & Soups, you can find everything from creamy dips to comforting soups, and all are ready in no time.

In Just Add Meat, you'll find recipes that contain everything except the fresh meat that can be added when you or whomever you give the jar to are ready to cook.

Pasta & Grains offers everything from Couscous with Figs and Almonds to Herb and Lemon Orzo with Peas.

The Beans & Legumes chapter was one of my favorites because in my house we eat a mostly vegetarian diet. You'll love the Curried Lentil Soup and the Tuscan Minestrone Soup.

Finally, round things out with Desserts & Drinks, a chapter featuring Mulled Wine, Spiced Chai, and of course, some delicious cakes and puddings!

I hope you have as much fun as I do creating beautiful layered jars of ready-to-eat meals to stock your cupboards and share with the people you love.

CHAPTER 1

Getting Started

There's something so satisfying about preparing a meal ahead of time, placing it carefully on the shelf, and knowing that at some point—maybe tomorrow, maybe next month—dinner is already taken care of. Nigella Lawson, chef and author of dozens of cookbooks, describes this as "putting up" in her book *How to Be a Domestic Goddess*.

As much as I love these traditional sensibilities, I'm also sensitive to the demands of modern life. It's not just charming and quaint to prepare meals ahead of time—it can be a necessity! We're doing more and moving faster than ever before.

Just as putting up is nothing new, neither is the concept of a pressure cooker. What is new is how easy it is to use. Thank goodness! Horror stories of exploding pots and scalded skin scared me into sticking with my usual stovetop, oven, and slow cooker routines until I found the Instant Pot.

This book has been a really fun change of pace from the type of cooking I usually do. While working with only fresh ingredients is lovely, it isn't always practical. Food goes bad. Beans take hours to soak. Moods change and what sounded great for dinner when I was planning my weekly menu later sounds unappetizing. Fortunately, with meals in jars, the shelf life is months, not days, and with the Instant Pot pressure cooker I can prepare whatever sounds good at that... well... at that instant!

Let's get started!

Equipment

You don't need a lot of fancy equipment to get started, just an Instant Pot pressure cooker and some inexpensive mason jars.

Instant Pot®

For the recipes in this book, I used the Instant Pot DUO Plus 60, 6 Quart 9-in-1 Multi-Use Programmable Pressure Cooker, Slow Cooker, Rice Cooker, Yogurt Maker, Egg Cooker, Sauté, Steamer, Warmer, and Sterilizer. I provide manual instructions for programming the Instant Pot, although you may rely on the pre-programmed options available if you wish. Refer to your Instant Pot setup guide to choose the pre-programmed options.

Jars

When I first started this project, I wanted to find the prettiest, most unique, modern glass jars. After exploring dozens of high-end options, I opted for the classic 1-quart Ball® mason jars for most of the recipes. They're inexpensive, easy to find, seal well to avoid spillage, and fit nicely together for storage. For a handful of recipes, I opted for smaller or sometimes larger jars as needed because they required fewer or more ingredients. Choose whatever brand you like, just ensure they're nearly the same size as what is specified in each recipe, or you will not be able to fit in all of the ingredients.

Ingredients

I chose to primarily include those ingredients I could easily find at my local grocery store. A handful are easier to find online, such as dried bell peppers, carrots, celery, and some of the more exotic spices.

Alternatively, consider dehydrating your own ingredients for each recipe. I wrote *The Ultimate Healthy Dehydrator Cookbook* in 2016 with instructions for dehydrating all of the vegetables used in this book.

Here are some of the more common ingredients that appear in this book.

Vegetables

Onion: Dried onion pieces are called for throughout the book. They're easy to find in the bulk spices section or in large plastic containers.

Garlic: Dried garlic pieces are called for throughout the book. They're easy to find in the bulk spices section or in large plastic containers. Occasionally, I also use garlic powder, which is also easy to find.

Carrots: Dried carrot pieces and dried shoestring carrots are used several times in the book. They're best sourced online or dried at home in a dehydrator or warm oven.

Celery: Dried celery pieces are used several times in the book. They're best sourced online or dried at home in a dehydrator or warm oven.

Bell pepper: Dried bell pepper pieces are used several times in the book. Red or green can be used unless a color is specified. They're best sourced online or dried at home in a dehydrator or warm oven.

Tomatoes: Sundried tomatoes are called for throughout the book. These should be air packed, *not packed in oil*. Choose tomatoes that do not have added herbs or spices unless you think they would complement whatever recipe you're preparing. They're easy to find in most grocery stores.

Kale: Dried kale is used in a couple recipes. Choose unflavored kale chips. Sea salt and olive oil are okay. They can also be dried in a dehydrator or warm oven.

Shelf Life

The shelf life of each prepared jar is roughly the length of the shortest shelf life of any of the ingredients contained therein. I go with three to six months as a general rule of thumb, though many recipes may last for several months longer. Nevertheless, look out for condensation on the inside of jars or mold growth, especially if you live in a humid environment. Shelf stable does not mean indefinite shelf life. Be especially watchful with ingredients that retain some moisture, such as dried figs, apricots, and tomatoes.

Because most of the ingredients in this book are shelf stable, most are also plant-based. This is good not only for our health but also for the planet. That said, you're welcome to add whatever fresh ingredients you like during the cooking process or as finishing ingredients.

Fruit

Figs: Dried figs are used throughout the book and are easily sourced in most grocery stores.

Apricots: Dried apricots are used throughout the book and are easily sourced in most grocery stores. Unsulphured is best.

Apples: Dried apples are used in a handful of recipes and are easily sourced in most grocery stores. Do not use apple chips. Unsulphured and organic are best.

Raisins: Raisins are used in a handful of recipes. Any variety is fine, but organic is best.

Citrus zest: Orange and lemon zest are used in a handful of recipes in this book. They can be purchased online or easily prepared at home in the oven. Use a Microplane grater to zest clean citrus and spread on a parchment-lined baking sheet. Dry for 30 minutes in a 200°F oven.

Legumes

Beans: Dry beans (kidney, pinto, cannellini, black, etc.) are used throughout this book. Source dry beans from grocery stores that have a lot of product turnover. Old beans take longer to cook. Sort all beans as you place them into the jars to remove any debris or sediment. The beans do not need to be soaked before cooking in the Instant Pot, but the cook times are significantly longer than if they had been soaked.

Dehydrated black beans are used once in the book and are easiest to find online. These are beans that have been fully cooked and cooled before drying. They cook in a minute or two in the Instant Pot.

Lentils: Red and green lentils are used throughout this book. Sort the lentils as you place them into the jars to remove any debris or sediment. You can even place them in a metal sieve and shake gently (without rinsing) to remove any light sediment.

Pasta and Grains

Pasta: Use dried pasta, not fresh, in all recipes that call for pasta. You can opt for gluten-free or whole-grain pastas, but it will affect the texture somewhat. Recipes were not tested with gluten-free pasta.

Grains: Rice, barley, polenta, quinoa, and other grains are used in many recipes in this book. Use the variety specified for best results. If you opt for a whole grain when a processed grain is called for, anticipate a slightly longer cooking time. Refer to your *Instant Pot Recipe Booklet* for guidance.

Use quick-cooking, pre-rinsed quinoa for best results.

Herbs and Spices

Chipotle: Ground chipotle is used in a couple recipes in this book. It is sometimes available in grocery stores in jars or in the bulk spices section. Alternatively, take whole dried chipotles and process in a spice mill until you get a fine powder. Do not use chipotle in adobo sauce.

Coriander: Ground coriander is used in many savory recipes in this book. It is widely available in grocery stores in jars and in the bulk spices section.

Cumin: Ground cumin is used in many savory recipes in this book. It is widely available in grocery stores in jars and in the bulk spices section.

Ginger: Both ground ginger and ginger pieces are used throughout the book. Ground ginger is easily sourced in most grocery stores. Ginger pieces can be found online. Do not confuse them with crystallized ginger candy.

Smoked paprika: Smoked paprika is used in many savory recipes in this book. It is available in many grocery stores in jars and online.

Broth

Vegetable, chicken, and beef broth are called for throughout the book. Choose a low-sodium broth whenever possible to avoid inadvertently over-salting the recipes. Alternatively, if you're making the jars for yourself and intend to use a heavily salted broth, omit the salt from the jar and season after cooking.

Instant Pot® Basics

This book assumes that you have a basic understanding of your Instant Pot, its settings, and handy accessories. If you don't already, just refer to the manual that came with your Instant Pot. Here are a couple specific directions for using this book to make meals in jars for your Instant Pot.

Sauté Function

Only the recipes in the Just Add Meat chapter and one other recipe call for using the sauté function. That is because the ingredients are shelf stable and require liquid for cooking.

Building Pressure

When you set the pressure-cooking time on your Instant Pot, it will take several minutes to build up pressure. This is not included in the cooking time, so plan your meal time accordingly.

Releasing Pressure

There are three ways to release pressure in the Instant Pot after cooking: quick release, natural release, and timed natural release. I use a combination of the natural release and timed natural release in this book.

Unless otherwise specified, here's what I recommend for most recipes: Allow the pressure to come down naturally for the time specified. Then carefully position the steam release valve on the lid to the "venting" position. If a significant amount of pressure remains in the pot, you should do this in short bursts to allow the steam to release but not emit the sauce.

Cooking Time

Sometimes the cooking time listed will be insufficient to fully cook a recipe. This can be due to a variety of factors, including the freshness of your ingredients. If the ingredients are not fully cooked after the specified cooking time has elapsed, simply place the lid back on the Instant Pot, turn the vent to the "sealed" position, and cook for another 5 to 10 minutes, or whatever time you estimate is required. This is a good option for cooking dried beans that are taking a long time to soften.

Alternatively, keep the lid off, turn the Instant Pot to the sauté function, and simmer until the ingredients are fully cooked. This allows some of the liquid to evaporate.

How to Make a Foil Sling

Newer versions of the Instant Pot come with a trivet with handles for lowering dishes into the pot. If you do not have one, make a foil sling. A foil sling can help you lower an additional cooking dish into the Instant Pot. To make one, roll out about 60 inches of heavy-duty aluminum foil. Fold it in half horizontally, so that it is now 30 inches long. Now fold it in thirds lengthwise so that it is extra thick. Place a baking dish in the center of the sling, lift from each end, and carefully lower the dish into the Instant Pot.

Special Diets

Many recipes comply with special diets, including gluten-free, allergen-free, vegan, and vegetarian. Gluten-free recipes contain no wheat, barley, rye, or other ingredients that contain gluten. Allergen-free recipes contain no wheat, dairy, soy, fish, shellfish, eggs, peanuts, or tree nuts. Vegan recipes contain no animal products such as meat, fish, dairy, eggs, or honey. Vegetarian recipes are free from meat and fish. If you do have any of these dietary restrictions, look for these designations in the recipes:

GF = Gluten Free   **V** = Vegetarian

AF = Allergen Free   **VGN** = Vegan

CHAPTER 2
Breakfast

Pumpkin Spice Steel-Cut Oats

This sweet breakfast porridge reminds me of my mother-in-law's pumpkin bread. It's delicious on cold winter mornings when you want nothing more than a comforting breakfast that didn't take hours to prepare.

Serves 4 to 6

Prep time: 5 minutes | **Cook time:** 15 minutes | **Release time:** 10 minutes
Jar size: 3 cups

VGN

Dry ingredients

1½ cups steel-cut oats

1 tablespoon pumpkin pie spice

¼ cup brown sugar

½ teaspoon sea salt

½ cup raisins

½ cup roughly chopped walnuts

For cooking and serving

6 cups water

1 cup pumpkin puree

Preparation: Layer the dry ingredients in the jar in the order listed.

To Cook: Place all of the jarred ingredients into the Instant Pot. Add 6 cups of water and the pumpkin puree. Stir to mix. Cover with the lid and ensure the vent is in the "sealed" position. Pressure cook on high for 15 minutes. Press Cancel. Allow the steam pressure to release naturally for 10 minutes, then release any remaining pressure manually.

Brown Sugar, Fig, and Pecan Steel-Cut Oats

Brown sugar, sweet dried figs, and pecans make a decadent morning meal and the perfect gift during the holiday season. You can substitute another dried fruit as well, such as cherry or apricot.

Serves 4 to 6

Prep time: 5 minutes | **Cook time:** 15 minutes | **Release time:** 10 minutes

Jar size: 3 cups

VGN

Dry ingredients

1½ cups steel-cut oats

¼ teaspoon ground nutmeg

⅓ cup brown sugar

½ teaspoon sea salt

½ cup pecan halves

½ cup halved dried figs

For cooking and serving

7 cups water

Preparation: Layer the dry ingredients in the jar in the order listed.

To Cook: Place all of the jarred ingredients into the Instant Pot. Add 7 cups of water. Stir to mix. Cover with the lid and ensure the vent is in the "sealed" position. Pressure cook on high for 15 minutes. Press Cancel. Allow the steam pressure to release naturally for 10 minutes, then release any remaining pressure manually.

Blueberry Almond Oats

Growing up in the Pacific Northwest, I went on backpacking trips with my family. One year our travels took us to Placid Lake in the Gifford Pinchot National Forest. The wilderness was beautiful and we set up camp in a field of wild blueberries. We picked them in the morning and served them over our packs of instant oatmeal. This recipe brings back all of those delicious memories.

Serves 4 to 6

Prep time: 5 minutes | **Cook time:** 5 minutes | **Release time:** 5 minutes

Jar size: 4 cups

VGN

Dry ingredients

¼ cup white sugar

½ teaspoon sea salt

2½ cups old-fashioned rolled oats

¾ cup dried blueberries

¼ cup toasted slivered almonds

For cooking and serving

5 cups water

Preparation: Layer the dry ingredients in the jar in the order listed.

To Cook: Place all of the jarred ingredients into the Instant Pot. Add 5 cups of water. Stir to mix. Cover with the lid and ensure the vent is in the "sealed" position. Pressure cook on high for 5 minutes. Press Cancel. Allow the steam pressure to release naturally for 5 minutes, then release any remaining pressure manually.

Tip: If you prefer a sugar-free option, you can simply omit the sugar or replace it with a nonnutritive sweetener such as stevia.

Latin Spiced Chocolate Quinoa

Chocolate and quinoa? It's not as crazy as it sounds. Both foods have ancient origins and figure prominently in regional cuisines throughout South America.

Serves 6

Prep time: 5 minutes | **Cook time:** 5 minutes | **Release time:** 5 minutes

Jar size: 2½ cups

GF | AF | VGN

Dry ingredients

¼ cup sugar

½ teaspoon sea salt

1½ cups quick-cooking quinoa

¼ cup unsweetened cocoa powder

½ teaspoon cinnamon

pinch cayenne pepper, optional

½ cup dark chocolate chips

For cooking and serving

4 cups water or unsweetened almond milk

Preparation: Layer the dry ingredients in the jar in the order listed.

To Cook: Place all of the jarred ingredients into the Instant Pot. Add 4 cups of water or almond milk. Stir to mix. Cover with the lid and ensure the vent is in the "sealed" position. Pressure cook on high for 5 minutes. Allow the steam pressure to release naturally for 5 minutes, then release any remaining pressure manually.

Ingredient Tip: You can use another kind of chili powder than cayenne, but make sure it only contains ground chiles, not onion powder, cumin, or other savory ingredients.

Cherry Buttermilk Coffee Cake

This dense and decadent breakfast cake is the perfect addition to a fancy brunch. Or, enjoy it with nothing more than a cup of coffee and a newspaper.

Serves 6 to 8

Prep time: 5 minutes | **Cook time:** 35 minutes | **Release time:** 10 minutes

Jar size: 3½ to 4 cups

V

Dry ingredients

¾ cup white sugar

½ teaspoon sea salt

2 teaspoons baking powder

¼ teaspoon baking soda

¼ cup buttermilk powder

1½ cups all-purpose flour

1 cup dried cherries

For cooking and serving

1 egg

1¼ cups water, divided

½ cup canola oil

cooking spray

Preparation: Layer the dry ingredients in the jar in the order listed.

To Cook: Place the egg, ¼ cup of water, and canola oil into a bowl, and stir to mix thoroughly. Add the jarred ingredients and mix until no lumps remain. Coat the interior of a 6-cup nonstick fluted tube pan, such as a Bundt pan, with cooking spray. Spread the cake batter into the tube pan and cover with aluminum foil.

Add the remaining 1 cup of water to the Instant Pot, then place the trivet in the bottom of the Instant Pot.

If needed, make a sling for the pan using the method described on page 12 and carefully lower the cake pan onto the trivet. Close the Instant Pot lid and ensure the vent is in the "sealed" position. Pressure cook on high for 35 minutes. Allow the steam pressure to release naturally for 10 minutes, then release any remaining pressure manually.

Carefully remove the tube pan using the sling and allow it to cool for about 15 minutes. Carefully invert the pan onto a plate and allow the cake to cool the rest of the way.

Cheesy Vegetable Strata

A strata is a crustless quiche that incorporates cubed or torn bread, making it the ultimate easy, one-pot breakfast recipe. This recipe makes it even simpler with dehydrated ingredients.

Serves 4

Prep time: 5 minutes | **Cook time:** 20 minutes | **Release time:** 10 minutes

Jar size: 5 cups

V

Dry ingredients

¼ cup dried Parmesan cheese

2 tablespoons dried yellow or green onion

¼ cup dried green bell pepper

2 tablespoons sundried tomatoes

1 tablespoon dried parsley

1 teaspoon sea salt

½ teaspoon ground black pepper

4 cups dry cubed bread

For cooking and serving

cooking spray

8 eggs

½ cup heavy cream

1 cup water

Preparation: Layer the dry ingredients in the jar in the order listed.

To Cook: Coat the bottom and sides of a 7-cup Pyrex dish or fluted tube pan, such as a Bundt pan, with cooking spray. Place all of the jarred ingredients into the baking dish.

In a separate jar, whisk the eggs and heavy cream. Pour this mixture into the pan, press down on the bread to submerge it beneath the egg mixture, and stir gently to disburse the ingredients. Cover the pan with aluminum foil.

Pour 1 cup of water into the Instant Pot and place the trivet into the pot. Use a foil sling (if needed) to place the baking dish on top of the trivet.

Cover the Instant Pot with the lid and ensure the vent is in the "sealed" position. Pressure cook on high for 20 minutes. Allow the steam pressure to release naturally for 10 minutes, then release any remaining pressure manually.

CHAPTER 3

Snacks, Sides, & Soups

Spicy Black Bean Dip

Whenever I'm running late with dinner, it's nice to have a healthy appetizer to snack on. This one is savory and offers protein and fiber from black beans blended with savory spices.

Serves 6 to 8

Prep time: 5 minutes | **Cook time:** 35 minutes | **Release time:** 20 minutes

Jar size: 4 cups

GF | AF | VGN

Dry ingredients

1 tablespoon chili powder

2 teaspoons ground cumin

1 tablespoon smoked paprika

1 teaspoon sea salt

1 teaspoon dried garlic

¼ cup dried onion

2 tablespoons dried green bell pepper

2 cups dried black beans

For cooking and serving

3½ cups vegetable broth or water, plus more as needed

¼ cup shredded mozzarella cheese, to serve, optional

diced green bell peppers, to serve

diced red onion, to serve

corn chips or raw vegetables, for dipping

Preparation: Layer the dry ingredients in the jar in the order listed.

To Cook: Place all of the jarred ingredients into the Instant Pot. Add 3½ cups of vegetable broth or water. Stir to mix. Cover with the lid and ensure the vent is in the "sealed" position. Pressure cook on high for 35 minutes. Allow the steam pressure to release naturally for 20 minutes. Use an immersion blender or carefully transfer the contents of the Instant Pot to a blender and puree until somewhat smooth, adding additional vegetable broth or water as needed to blend.

To Serve: Pour the mixture into a serving dish and top with the shredded cheese, if using. Top with diced bell peppers and onions, and serve with corn chips or raw vegetables.

Gluten-Free Vegan Quinoa Dressing

This is my go-to recipe for vegans at Thanksgiving, adapted for the Instant Pot from the food blog, Healthy Seasonal Recipes. It offers protein and complex carbohydrates from quinoa, pecans, and kale, so everyone can enjoy a complete meal.

Serves 4 to 6

Prep time: 5 minutes | **Cook time:** 10 minutes | **Release time:** 5 minutes

Jar size: 4 cups

GF | **VGN**

Dry ingredients

1¾ cups quinoa

¼ cup dried onion

1 teaspoon dried garlic

¼ cup dried celery

2 teaspoons dried sage

1 teaspoon dried thyme

½ teaspoon sea salt

¼ teaspoon ground cinnamon

½ cup dried cranberries

¼ cup roughly chopped pecans

1 cup dried kale

For cooking and serving

2 tablespoons olive oil

3 cups vegetable broth

Preparation: Layer the dry ingredients in the jar in the order listed.

To Cook: Add the olive oil to the Instant Pot, and brush to coat the bottom and sides of the pot. Place all of the jarred ingredients into the Instant Pot. Add 3 cups of vegetable broth. Stir to mix. Cover with the lid and ensure the vent is in the "sealed" position. Pressure cook on low for 10 minutes. Allow the steam pressure to release naturally for 5 minutes, then release any remaining pressure manually.

Fluff with a fork before serving.

Traditional Holiday Dressing

Forget cooking the holiday dressing inside a turkey—make it in the Instant Pot. Not only is this a safer method of cooking, you can also make a lot more. Give this as a hostess gift and save your host the challenge of making yet another side dish.

Serves 4

Prep time: 5 minutes | **Cook time:** 10 minutes | **Release time:** 5 minutes
Jar size: 7 cups

Dry ingredients

⅓ cup dried onion

¼ cup dried celery

2 teaspoons dried sage

1 teaspoon dried thyme

½ teaspoon sea salt

¼ cup dried cranberries

¼ cup minced dried apples

6 cups dry cubed bread

For cooking and serving

¼ cup butter, melted

3 cups chicken broth or vegetable broth

Preparation: Layer the dry ingredients in the jar in the order listed.

To Cook: Add the butter to the Instant Pot, and brush to coat the bottom and sides of the pot. Place all of the jarred ingredients into the Instant Pot. Add 3 cups chicken or vegetable broth. Stir to mix. Cover with the lid and ensure the vent is in the "sealed" position. Pressure cook on low for 10 minutes. Allow the steam pressure to release naturally for 5 minutes, then release any remaining pressure manually.

Fluff with a fork before serving.

Ingredient Tip: To make this dish vegetarian, use vegetable broth.

Cheesy Herbed Polenta

Polenta is often considered a labor-intensive dish that requires constant attention to continue stirring throughout the 30-minute stovetop cooking time. However, I recently began using a different technique to cook polenta, covering it and letting it cook unattended, save a few occasional stirs. It turned out so well, I knew the grain would be perfect in the Instant Pot, where it takes even less effort. It's a delicious accompaniment to a whole roasted chicken and blanched vegetables.

Serves 4 to 6

Prep time: 5 minutes | **Cook time:** 15 minutes | **Release time:** 10 minutes
Jar size: 2½ cups

GF

Dry ingredients

2 cups polenta

½ teaspoon sea salt

1 tablespoon dried Italian herb blend

¼ cup dried Parmesan cheese

For cooking and serving

8 cups chicken broth or water

2 tablespoons butter, optional

Preparation: Layer the dry ingredients in the jar in the order listed.

To Cook: Place all of the jarred ingredients into the Instant Pot. Add 8 cups of chicken broth or water. Stir to mix. Cover with the lid and ensure the vent is in the "sealed" position. Pressure cook on high for 10 minutes. Manually release the steam pressure. Remove the lid and stir thoroughly. Cover with the lid once again and place the vent into the "sealed" position. Pressure cook on high for another 5 minutes. Allow the pressure to release naturally for 10 minutes, then release any remaining pressure manually. Stir in the butter, if using.

Ingredient Tip: To make this dish vegetarian, substitute the chicken broth with water.

Cream of Mushroom Soup

Mushrooms are one of my go-to replacements for meat because they're just loaded with umami flavors and they have a nice meaty texture. Dried thyme and parsley add further dimensions of flavor to this comforting soup.

Serves 4 to 6

Prep time: 5 minutes | **Cook time:** 10 minutes | **Release time:** 10 minutes

Jar size: 3 cups

GF

Dry ingredients

⅓ cup dried onion

2 tablespoons dried celery

1 teaspoon dried garlic

1 teaspoon sea salt

2 teaspoons dried thyme

1 tablespoon dried parsley

2 cups assorted dried mushrooms

For cooking and serving

6 cups chicken broth or water

¼ cup dry white wine, optional

½ cup heavy cream

Preparation: Layer dry the ingredients in the jar in the order listed.

To Cook: Place all of the jarred ingredients into the Instant Pot. Add 6 cups of chicken broth or water and the white wine, if using. Stir to mix. Cover with the lid and ensure the vent is in the "sealed" position. Pressure cook on high for 10 minutes. Allow the steam pressure to release naturally for 10 minutes, then release any remaining pressure manually. Stir in the heavy cream.

Ingredient Tip: I prefer wild mushrooms and a blend of shiitake and some porcini. Go easy on the porcini, though, because the flavor can be really intense. To make this dish vegetarian, substitute the chicken broth with water.

Creamy Corn Chowder

This corn chowder starts out with one of the fundamental elements of French cooking—mirepoix. It is a blend of onion, carrots, and celery, and while fresh is best, the dried vegetables are also good. Mashed potato flakes and heavy cream make this soup especially creamy.

Serves 4 to 6

Prep time: 5 minutes | **Cook time:** 10 minutes | **Release time:** 5 minutes

Jar size: 3 cups

GF | AF | V

Dry Ingredients

¼ cup mashed potato flakes

¼ cup dried onions

2 tablespoons dried carrots

2 tablespoons dried celery

1 teaspoon sea salt

1 teaspoon dried thyme

2 cups dried corn kernels

For cooking and serving

8 cups vegetable broth or water

1 teaspoon white wine vinegar

½ cup heavy cream

Preparation: Layer the dry ingredients in the jar in the order listed.

To Cook: Place all of the jarred ingredients into the Instant Pot. Add 8 cups of vegetable broth or water. Stir to mix. Cover with the lid and ensure the vent is in the "sealed" position. Pressure cook on high for 10 minutes. Allow the steam pressure to release naturally for 5 minutes, then release any remaining pressure manually. Stir in the white wine vinegar, then stir in the heavy cream.

Tom Yum Soup

I have to apologize in advance—you're not going to find many of these ingredients in your local grocery store unless you're lucky enough to live near an Asian market. But it's worth the effort to buy them online! Fragrant kaffir lime leaves, spicy galangal, pungent dried shrimp, and savory mushrooms permeate a creamy coconut broth in this traditional Southeast Asian soup.

Serves 4

Prep time: 5 minutes | **Cook time:** 10 minutes | **Release time:** 10 minutes

Jar size: 2 cups

GF

Dry ingredients

¼ cup dried onion

2 tablespoons dried green onion

1 teaspoon dried garlic

¼ teaspoon sea salt

1 tablespoon brown sugar

1 tablespoon dried shrimp

½ cup sliced dried shiitake mushrooms

2 tablespoons sundried tomatoes

4 pieces dried galangal

4 dried kaffir lime leaves

2 dried chiles, such as chile de arbol

For cooking and serving

1 (12-ounce) can full-fat coconut milk

8 cups chicken broth or vegetable broth

1 to 2 limes, halved, to serve

fresh cilantro, roughly chopped, to serve

Preparation: Layer the dry ingredients in the jar in the order listed.

To Cook: Place all of the jarred ingredients into the Instant Pot. Add the coconut milk and broth. Stir to mix. Cover with the lid and ensure the vent is in the "sealed" position. Pressure cook on high for 10 minutes. Allow the steam pressure to release naturally for 10 minutes, then release any remaining pressure manually.

To Serve: Season to taste with lime juice and garnish with fresh cilantro.

Tomato Basil Soup

Sure, you could buy tomato soup in a can or carton, but with all of the ingredients in a jar, you can make a fresh batch in just a few extra minutes.

Serves 4

Prep time: 5 minutes | **Cook time:** 5 minutes | **Release time:** 10 minutes

Jar size: 3½ to 4 cups

GF | **AF** | **VGN**

Dry ingredients

½ teaspoon sea salt

½ cup dried carrots

½ cup dried onion

2 tablespoons dried basil

2 cups sundried tomatoes

For cooking and serving

8 cups vegetable broth or water

¼ cup extra-virgin olive oil

Preparation: Layer the dry ingredients in the jar in the order listed.

To Cook: Place all of the jarred ingredients into the Instant Pot. Add 8 cups of vegetable broth or water. Stir to mix. Cover with the lid and ensure the vent is in the "sealed" position. Pressure cook on high for 5 minutes. Allow the steam pressure to release naturally for 10 minutes, then release any remaining pressure manually. Use an immersion blender or carefully transfer the soup to a blender (be sure to vent and cover with a cloth). Puree until completely smooth. With the blender running, pour in the olive oil until emulsified.

CHAPTER 4

Just Add Meat

Homestyle Beef Chili

When fall rolls around, nothing is quite as comforting as snuggling under a wool blanket and watching football outside with a steaming bowl of chili in one hand and a cold dark beer in the other. So, I highly recommend packing this meal in a jar with all of the above—maybe even tickets to the game! The chili can be kept vegetarian, if that's your thing. Just skip the first cooking steps and use vegetable broth.

Serves 8

Prep time: 5 minutes | **Cook time:** 45 minutes | **Release time:** 15 minutes

Jar size: 3¼ to 4 cups

GF | AF

Dry ingredients

1 tablespoon ground cumin	½ cup dried onion
1 tablespoon smoked paprika	1 tablespoon dried garlic
1 tablespoon chili powder	½ cup dried bell pepper
1 teaspoon sea salt	2 cups dried red kidney beans
¼ cup sundried tomatoes	

For cooking and serving

1 pound ground beef	8 cups beef broth

Preparation: Layer the dry ingredients in the jar in the order listed.

To Cook: Select sauté to preheat the Instant Pot. When the word "hot" appears on the display, crumble the beef into the pot and cook for 5 minutes. Place all of the jarred ingredients into the Instant Pot. Add the beef broth. Stir to mix. Cover with the lid and ensure the vent is in the "sealed" position. Pressure cook on high for 45 minutes. Allow the steam pressure to release naturally for 15 minutes, then release any remaining pressure manually.

Ingredient Tip: Look for a good-quality chili powder without added salt. It should have a blend of ground chiles as well as additional herbs and spices.

Moroccan Lamb Tagine

This tagine is adapted from Lemonade, one of my favorite restaurants in Los Angeles. Thanks to the Instant Pot, it's ready in a fraction of the time of the original recipe.

Serves 6 to 8

Prep time: 5 minutes | **Cook time:** 25 minutes | **Release time:** 10 minutes
Jar size: 3 cups

GF | **AF**

Dry ingredients

2 tablespoons ground ginger	2 tablespoons brown sugar
1 tablespoon ground cumin	¼ cup dried onion
1 tablespoon ground turmeric	¼ cup dried carrots
1 teaspoon allspice	¼ cup dried celery
1 teaspoon ground cinnamon	½ cup sliced dried apricots
½ teaspoon cayenne pepper	½ cup sliced dried figs
½ teaspoon sea salt	½ cup toasted slivered almonds

For cooking and serving

2 tablespoons canola oil	sea salt and pepper
2 pounds boneless lamb shoulder, cut into 1-inch cubes	4 cups chicken or vegetable broth

Preparation: Layer the dry ingredients in the jar in the order listed.

To Cook: Select sauté to preheat the Instant Pot. When the word "hot" appears on the display, add the oil. It should thin immediately. Pat the lamb cubes dry with paper towels and season generously with salt and pepper, then sear in the Instant Pot until browned on all sides, about 10 minutes.

Add all of the jarred ingredients to the Instant Pot, along with the broth. Stir to mix. Cover with the lid and ensure the vent is in the "sealed" position. Pressure cook on high for 15 minutes. Allow the steam pressure to release naturally for 10 minutes, then release any remaining pressure manually.

Wild Rice with Chorizo

This flavorful meal makes a filling entrée with a dark leafy green salad and a bottle of dry red wine. Smoky, spicy chorizo permeates the wild rice while dried cranberries add a touch of sweetness and pungent rosemary rounds out the dish.

Serves 4 to 6

Prep time: 5 minutes | **Cook time:** 30 minutes | **Release time:** 10 minutes

Jar size: 2¾ to 3 cups

GF | AF

Dry ingredients

¼ cup dried onion

1 teaspoon dried garlic

2 tablespoons dried celery

1 tablespoon dried rosemary

½ teaspoon sea salt

2 cups wild rice

¼ cup dried cranberries

For cooking and serving

1 pound pork chorizo

4 cups chicken broth

Preparation: Layer the dry ingredients in the jar in the order listed.

To Cook: Select sauté to preheat the Instant Pot. When the word "hot" appears on the display, crumble the chorizo into the pot, breaking it up with a spoon. It will release some fat and begin to brown slightly. Cook for 5 minutes.

Add all of the jarred ingredients to the Instant Pot along with the chicken broth. Stir to mix. Cover with the lid and ensure the vent is in the "sealed" position. Pressure cook on high for 25 minutes. Allow the steam pressure to release naturally for 10 minutes, then release any remaining pressure manually.

Beef Barley Soup

Pearl barley, herbs, and garden vegetables make this soup a healthy one-pot meal—just add beef. I like to deglaze the pot with a bit of red wine, but that's totally optional.

Serves 4 to 6

Prep time: 5 minutes | **Cook time:** 32 minutes | **Release time:** 10 minutes
Jar size: 3 cups

AF

Dry ingredients

¼ cup dried carrots

½ cup dried onion

2 tablespoons dried celery

1 teaspoon dried garlic

1 teaspoon dried thyme

1 teaspoon dried rosemary

1 tablespoon dried parsley

2 cups dried pearl barley

¼ teaspoon sea salt

For cooking and serving

2 tablespoons canola oil

1 pound beef chuck, cut into 1-inch cubes

sea salt and pepper

¼ cup red wine, optional

8 cups beef broth

Preparation: Layer the dry ingredients in the jar in the order listed.

To Cook: Select sauté to preheat the Instant Pot. When the word "hot" appears on the display, add the oil. It should thin immediately. Pat the beef dry with paper towels and season generously with salt and pepper. Sear the beef in the Instant Pot until it is gently browned on all sides, about 10 minutes. Add the red wine, if using, and scrape up any browned bits from the bottom of the pot.

Add all of the jarred ingredients to the Instant Pot along with the 8 cups of beef broth. Stir to mix. Cover with the lid and ensure the vent is in the "sealed" position. Pressure cook on high for 22 minutes. Allow the steam pressure to release naturally for 10 minutes, then release any remaining pressure manually.

Tip: Although this recipe is allergen free, it is not gluten free because it contains barley. For a gluten-free option, use brown rice or wild rice and cook for the same amount of time.

Posole

In the Instant Pot, pork shoulder becomes as tender as if it had been simmered for hours in this classic Mexican soup. The amount of broth may seem like a lot, but it is designed to be a thinner soup. This posole is served with cilantro, radishes, avocado, and lime juice.

Serves 6 to 8

Prep time: 5 minutes | **Cook time:** 40 minutes | **Release time:** 15 minutes

Jar size: 3 cups

GF | AF

Dry ingredients

1 tablespoon chile de arbol

1 tablespoon ancho chile powder

2 teaspoons ground cumin

1 tablespoon dried Mexican oregano

¼ teaspoon sea salt

2 teaspoons dried garlic

⅓ cup dried onion

1 bay leaf

2 cups dried hominy

For cooking and serving

2 tablespoons canola oil

1½ pounds pork shoulder, cut into 2-inch pieces

salt and pepper

12 cups chicken broth

1 cup roughly chopped cilantro, to serve

1 bunch radishes, thinly sliced, to serve

2 avocados, diced, to serve

2 limes, cut into wedges, to serve

Preparation: Layer the dry ingredients in the jar in the order listed.

To Cook: Select sauté to preheat the Instant Pot. When the word "hot" appears on the display, add the oil. It should thin immediately. Pat the pork shoulder dry with paper towels and season generously with salt and pepper. Sear the pork in the Instant Pot until browned on all sides, about 10 minutes.

Add all of the jarred ingredients to the Instant Pot along with the 12 cups of broth. Stir to mix. Cover with the lid and ensure the vent is in the "sealed" position. Pressure cook on high for 30 minutes. Allow the steam pressure to release naturally for 15 minutes, then release any remaining pressure manually.

To Serve: Divide the soup between serving bowls and top with chopped cilantro, sliced radishes, and diced avocado. Finish with a squeeze of lime juice.

Tip: Dried hominy is similar to dried beans insofar as it is typically soaked and then cooked to rehydrate it. Soaking is not essential, though. And, cooking it in this rich, flavorful broth infuses the grain with flavor.

Ginger Beef Noodle Soup

Fragrant ginger and star anise liven up this basic beef and noodle soup.

Serves 4 to 6

Prep time: 5 minutes | **Cook time:** 35 minutes | **Release time:** 10 minutes
Jar size: 4 cups

Dry ingredients

1 tablespoon uncrystallized dried ginger slices or 2 teaspoons ground ginger

¼ cup dried onion

1 star anise pod

1 pinch red chile flakes

¼ teaspoon sea salt

½ cup chopped dried shiitake mushrooms

8 ounces Chinese-style soba noodles or plain spaghetti, broken into pieces

For cooking and serving

2 tablespoons canola oil

1½ pounds beef chuck, cut into 1-inch pieces

sea salt and pepper

8 cups beef broth

2 tablespoons soy sauce, or to taste

Preparation: Layer the dry ingredients in the jar in the order listed.

To Cook: Select sauté to preheat the Instant Pot. When the word "hot" appears on the display, add the oil. It should thin immediately. Pat the beef dry with paper towels and season generously with salt and pepper. Sear the beef in the Instant Pot until browned on all sides, about 10 minutes. Add the beef broth to the pot.

Cover the pot with the lid and ensure the vent is in the "sealed" position. Pressure cook on high for 20 minutes. Allow the steam pressure to release naturally for 10 minutes, then release any remaining pressure manually.

Add all of the jarred ingredients to the Instant Pot. Stir to mix. Using the sauté function, simmer for 10 minutes, until the noodles are al dente and the mushrooms have softened. Stir in the soy sauce to taste.

Spicy Tortilla Soup

Ready in an instant, this flavorful tortilla soup makes an easy weeknight supper—just add chicken.

Serves 4

Prep time: 5 minutes | **Cook time:** 10 minutes | **Release time:** 5 minutes

Jar size: 3 cups

GF | AF

Dry ingredients

1 tablespoon paprika

2 teaspoons ground cumin

1 teaspoon ground coriander

1 tablespoon chili powder

1 teaspoon sea salt

¼ cup sundried tomatoes

¼ cup dried onion

½ cup dried corn

1 teaspoon dried garlic

1 cup tortilla strips

For cooking and serving

2 tablespoons canola oil

1 pound boneless skinless chicken thighs, cut into 1-inch pieces

salt and pepper

8 cups chicken broth

1 lime, halved, to serve

1 avocado, sliced, to serve

tortilla strips, to serve

Preparation: Layer the dry ingredients in the jar in the order listed.

To Cook: Select sauté to preheat the Instant Pot. When the word "hot" appears on the display, add the oil. It should thin immediately. Pat the chicken dry with paper towels and season generously with salt and pepper. Sear the chicken in the Instant Pot for 5 minutes.

Add all of the jarred ingredients to the Instant Pot along with the 8 cups of broth. Stir to mix. Cover with the lid and ensure the vent is in the "sealed" position. Pressure cook on high for 5 minutes. Allow the steam pressure to release naturally for 5 minutes, then release any remaining pressure manually.

To Serve: Finish with a squeeze of lime juice and top with avocado and additional tortilla strips.

CHAPTER 5

Pasta & Grains

Jade Rice Congee with Shiitake Mushrooms

Jade rice gets its gorgeous green hue from bamboo juice. Although the color fades somewhat during cooking, it imparts a subtly sweet flavor and lovely creamy texture to congee, an Asian-style rice porridge. It is complemented by the umami richness of shiitake mushrooms and hint of ginger and garlic.

Serves 4 to 6

Prep time: 5 minutes | **Cook time:** 10 minutes | **Release time:** 10 minutes

Jar size: 4 cups

GF | AF | VGN

Dry ingredients

2½ cups jade pearl rice	1 teaspoon ground ginger
¼ cup dried onion	½ teaspoon sea salt
1 teaspoon dried garlic	1 cup dried shiitake mushrooms, halved

For cooking and serving

12 cups vegetable broth or water	soy sauce, to serve
green onions, thinly sliced, to serve	

Preparation: Layer the dry ingredients in the jar in the order listed.

To Cook: Place all of the jarred ingredients into the Instant Pot. Add 12 cups of vegetable broth or water. Stir to mix. Cover with the lid and ensure the vent is in the "sealed" position. Pressure cook on high for 10 minutes. Press Cancel and allow the steam pressure to release naturally for 10 minutes, then release any remaining pressure manually.

To Serve: Top with fresh green onions and soy sauce to taste.

Herb and Lemon Orzo with Peas

Parsley, thyme, and lemon are the stars of this simple vegan pasta dish.

Serves 4

Prep time: 5 minutes | **Cook time:** 5 minutes | **Release time:** 5 minutes

Jar size: 4 cups

VGN

Dry ingredients

2½ cups dry orzo pasta

½ teaspoon sea salt

1 tablespoon dried parsley

1 teaspoon dried thyme

1 teaspoon dried garlic

1 teaspoon dried lemon zest

1 cup dehydrated peas

For cooking and serving

4 cups vegetable broth or water

2 tablespoons extra-virgin olive oil

Preparation: Layer the dry ingredients in the jar in the order listed.

To Cook: Place all of the jarred ingredients into the Instant Pot. Add 4 cups of vegetable broth or water. Stir to mix. Cover with the lid and ensure the vent is in the "sealed" position. Pressure cook on high for 5 minutes. Allow the steam pressure to release naturally for 5 minutes, then release any remaining pressure manually.

Tortellini with Sundried Tomato and Basil

Cooking pasta in the Instant Pot not only gives you a tasty one-pot meal, but it also means no draining pasta water. Onion, garlic, herbs, and sundried tomatoes liven up cheese tortellini. Feel free to use whatever shelf-stable pasta you like.

Serves 4

Prep time: 5 minutes | **Cook time:** 5 minutes | **Release time:** 5 minutes
Jar size: 4 cups

V

Dry ingredients

¼ cup dried onions

1 teaspoon dried garlic

½ teaspoon sea salt

1 tablespoon dried basil

1 tablespoon dried parsley

½ cup sundried tomatoes

10 ounces dried cheese-filled tortellini

For cooking and serving

6 cups vegetable broth or water

Preparation: Layer the dry ingredients in the jar in the order listed.

To Cook: Place all of the jarred ingredients into the Instant Pot. Add 6 cups of vegetable broth or water. Stir to mix. Cover with the lid and ensure the vent is in the "sealed" position. Pressure cook on high for 5 minutes. Allow the steam pressure to release naturally for 5 minutes, then release any remaining pressure manually.

Smoky Chipotle Quinoa, Black Beans, and Corn

Technically, quinoa isn't a grain at all; it's a seed. But who really cares? The ancient South American staple is loaded with complex carbs and protein. Coupled with black beans and corn, it makes a complete, plant-based meal.

Serves 6

Prep time: 5 minutes | **Cook time:** 5 minutes | **Release time:** 5 minutes

Jar size: 4 cups

GF | AF | VGN

Dry ingredients

1 tablespoon ground chipotle powder

2 teaspoons ground cumin

2 tablespoons dried onion

1 teaspoon dried garlic

1 teaspoon Mexican oregano

¼ teaspoon sea salt

2 cups quick-cooking quinoa

1 cup dehydrated black beans

½ cup dried corn

For cooking and serving

4 cups vegetable broth or water

roughly chopped fresh cilantro, to serve

lime juice, to serve

Preparation: Layer the dry ingredients in the jar in the order listed.

To Cook: Place all of the jarred ingredients into the Instant Pot. Add 4 cups of broth or water. Stir to mix. Cover with the lid and ensure the vent is in the "sealed" position. Pressure cook on high for 5 minutes. Allow the steam pressure to release naturally for 5 minutes, then release any remaining pressure manually.

To Serve: Garnish with fresh cilantro and a squeeze of lime juice.

Ingredient Tip: Make sure to use precooked, dehydrated black beans. They should not be confused with dry black beans, which require a much longer cooking time.

Biryani

Biryani is a seasoned rice dish served throughout the Middle East, India, and Bangladesh. Hence, it has regional variations that differ wildly. This one is a vegan version, but if you like, you can sauté one pound of chicken, beef, or lamb for 10 minutes in the Instant Pot before proceeding with the recipe.

Serves 4 to 6

Prep time: 5 minutes | **Cook time:** 4 minutes | **Release time:** 10 minutes

Jar size: 4 cups

GF | AF | VGN

Dry ingredients

½ teaspoon cardamom

½ teaspoon ground coriander

¼ teaspoon cayenne pepper

1 tablespoon garam masala

pinch of saffron

⅓ cup dried onion

2 tablespoons dried green bell pepper

1 teaspoon dried garlic

1 teaspoon ground ginger

½ teaspoon sea salt

2½ cups long-grain basmati rice

½ cup raisins

For cooking and serving

2½ cups vegetable broth or water

Preparation: Layer the dry ingredients in the jar in the order listed.

To Cook: Place all of the jarred ingredients into the Instant Pot. Add 2½ cups of vegetable broth or water. Stir to mix. Cover with the lid and ensure the vent is in the "sealed" position. Select the rice function and cook for 4 minutes. Allow the steam pressure to release naturally for 10 minutes, then release any remaining pressure manually.

Garden Vegetable Millet Pilaf

I grew up eating millet for breakfast. My brothers and I called it birdseed, and it does have a perfectly round shape reminiscent of birdseed. But it's hearty and loaded with protein, making it a healthy side dish.

Serves 6 to 8

Prep time: 5 minutes | **Cook time:** 12 minutes | **Release time:** 10 minutes

Jar size: 4 cups

GF | AF | VGN

Dry ingredients

3 cups millet

¼ cup dried onion

¼ cup dried carrots

¼ cup dried zucchini

2 tablespoons thinly sliced sundried tomatoes

1 teaspoon dried garlic

1 tablespoon herbes de Provence

½ teaspoon dried lemon zest

1 teaspoon sea salt

For cooking and serving

4 cups vegetable broth or water

Preparation: Layer the dry ingredients in the jar in the order listed.

To Cook: Place all of the jarred ingredients into the Instant Pot. Add 4 cups of vegetable broth or water. Stir to mix. Cover with the lid and ensure the vent is in the "sealed" position. Pressure cook on high for 12 minutes. Allow the steam pressure to release naturally for 10 minutes, then release any remaining pressure manually.

Tabbouleh

This Middle Eastern salad is best enjoyed at room temperature or chilled. If you're in a hurry, you can prepare it as directed and then spread on a sheet pan to cool. This is how professional chefs cool cooked foods so that the temperature drops quickly and they don't overcook.

Serves 4

Prep time: 5 minutes | **Cook time:** 12 minutes | **Release time:** 0 minutes

Jar size: 3½ to 4 cups

VGN

Dry ingredients

2 cups bulgur wheat

¼ cup sundried tomatoes

½ cup dried parsley

¼ cup dried mint

½ teaspoon sea salt

¼ cup dried green onions

For cooking and serving

4 cups water

¼ cup lemon juice, to serve

¼ cup olive oil, to serve

Preparation: Layer the dry ingredients in the jar in the order listed.

To Cook: Place all of the jarred ingredients into the Instant Pot. Add 4 cups of vegetable broth or water. Stir to mix. Cover with the lid and ensure the vent is in the "sealed" position. Select the rice function and pressure cook on low for 12 minutes. Use manual pressure release.

To Serve: Stir in the lemon juice and olive oil.

Couscous with Figs and Almonds

This simple side dish is delicious served warm or chilled. I like to take it to the beach for picnics or serve it warm alongside a roast in the late fall.

Serves 4 to 6

Prep time: 5 minutes | **Cook time:** 3 minutes | **Release time:** 5 minutes

Jar size: 3 cups

VGN

Dry ingredients

2 cups couscous

2 tablespoons dried onion

1 teaspoon dried mint

¼ teaspoon dried cinnamon

1 teaspoon sea salt

½ cup sliced dried figs

½ cup slivered toasted almonds

For cooking and serving

4 cups vegetable broth or water

Preparation: Layer the dry ingredients in the jar in the order listed.

To Cook: Place all of the jarred ingredients into the Instant Pot. Add 4 cups of vegetable broth or water. Stir to mix. Cover with the lid and ensure the vent is in the "sealed" position. Pressure cook on high for 3 minutes. Allow the steam pressure to release naturally for 5 minutes, then release any remaining pressure manually.

Saffron Rice with Tahdig

Tahdig (TAH-deeg) is the buttery, crispy, crunchy layer of rice that forms at the bottom of the pan in this savory Persian dish.

Serves 4 to 6

Prep time: 5 minutes | **Cook time:** 12 to 14 minutes | **Release time:** 10 minutes

Jar size: 2½ cups

GF | V

Dry ingredients

2 cups basmati rice

1 teaspoon saffron threads, gently crushed

2 tablespoons dried parsley

2 tablespoons dried mint

1 teaspoon dried dill

1 teaspoon sea salt

For cooking and serving

2 tablespoons olive oil

2¼ cups water

¼ cup butter, melted

Preparation: Layer the dry ingredients in the jar in the order listed.

To Cook: Coat the bottom and sides of the Instant Pot with the olive oil. Place all of the jarred ingredients into the Instant Pot. Add 2¼ cups of water. Stir gently to mix. Cover with the lid and ensure the vent is in the "sealed" position. Select the rice function and cook for 4 minutes. Release the pressure manually and then drape a clean kitchen towel over the rice to continue steaming it for 10 minutes.

Turn on the sauté function. Poke four holes into the rice with the bottom of a wooden spoon and pour the melted butter into the holes and around the edges. Cook for another 8 to 10 minutes without stirring.

To Serve: Remove the pot from the machine using pot holders. Use a spatula to carefully loosen the rice from the sides of the pot. Place a platter on top of the pot and carefully invert. If some of the rice sticks to the bottom of the pot, no worries, just scoop it up and place it crisp-side up on the platter.

CHAPTER 6
Beans & Legumes

Chipotle Black Bean Soup

The smoky sweetness of chipotle chile adds depth of flavor to every dish it touches—the kind of flavor that makes you say, "What is in this?!" Chipotles are smoke-dried jalapeno peppers and can be purchased canned in adobo sauce, but because we're using them in a jar, opt for the dried, ground variety.

Serves 6 to 8

Prep time: 5 minutes | **Cook time:** 30 minutes | **Release time:** 20 minutes

Jar size: 4 cups

GF | AF | VGN

Dry ingredients

1 tablespoon ground chipotle

2 teaspoons ground cumin

2 teaspoons smoked paprika

1 teaspoon sea salt

1 teaspoon dried garlic

⅓ cup dried onion

2 tablespoons dried green bell pepper

3 cups dried black beans

For cooking and serving

6 cups vegetable broth or water

Preparation: Layer the dry ingredients in the jar in the order listed.

To Cook: Place all of the jarred ingredients into the Instant Pot. Add 6 cups of vegetable broth or water. Stir to mix. Cover with the lid and ensure the vent is in the "sealed" position. Pressure cook on high for 30 minutes. Allow the steam pressure to release naturally for 20 minutes.

Ingredient Tip: If you cannot find chipotle powder, purchase the chipotles whole and process them in a spice grinder or clean coffee grinder. You can find the whole chiles in the bulk spices or Mexican foods aisle of a well-stocked grocery store.

Frijoles de la Olla

Sweet pinto beans simmered in a rich, garlicky broth are comforting and make a delicious complete meal. I adapted the recipe from vegan chef Roberto Martin's book, *Vegan Cooking for Carnivores*. Preparing the meal in a jar ahead of time makes it really easy to whip up this dish. It borders on a soup, which I love, and gets better after it sits for a while.

Serves 6 to 8

Prep time: 5 minutes | **Cook time:** 30 minutes | **Release time:** 20 minutes
Jar size: 3½ to 4 cups

GF | AF | VGN

Dry ingredients

1 teaspoon sea salt

2 tablespoons dried garlic

⅓ cup dried onion

2 teaspoons dried Mexican oregano

3 cups dried pinto beans

For cooking and serving

6 cups vegetable broth or water

Preparation: Layer the dry ingredients in the jar in the order listed.

To Cook: Place all of the jarred ingredients into the Instant Pot. Add 6 cups of vegetable broth or water. Stir to mix. Cover with the lid and ensure the vent is in the "sealed" position. Pressure cook on high for 30 minutes. Allow the steam pressure to release naturally for 20 minutes.

Serving Tip: These beans are especially delicious when contrasted with a fresh pico de gallo salsa and sliced avocado or sour cream.

Traveler's Special Split Pea Soup

About half an hour up the coast from where I live in Santa Barbara, California, lies Anderson's Restaurant, which prides itself on its pea soup, serving more than 2 million bowls a year. There's something so cozy about driving up the Central Coast and stopping in for a steaming bowl. I also really appreciate that they offer a completely vegetarian soup—a rare find. When I'm staying closer to home, I try to recreate their soup, and it comes pretty close!

Serves 6 to 8

Prep time: 5 minutes | **Cook time:** 20 minutes | **Release time:** 15 minutes

Jar size: 4 cups

GF | AF | VGN

Dry ingredients

⅓ cup dried onion

1 teaspoon dried garlic

¼ cup dried celery

2 dried bay leaves

1 teaspoon dried thyme

1 teaspoon smoked sea salt

3 cups dried green split peas

For cooking and serving

6 cups vegetable broth or water

Preparation: Layer the dry ingredients in the jar in the order listed.

To Cook: Place all of the jarred ingredients into the Instant Pot. Add 6 cups of vegetable broth or water. Stir to mix. Cover with the lid and ensure the vent is in the "sealed" position. Pressure cook on high for 20 minutes. Allow the steam pressure to release naturally for 15 minutes, then release any remaining pressure manually.

Ingredient Tip: Regular sea salt is acceptable in place of the smoked sea salt, but if you have it, it lends a nice smoky component to this naturally vegan recipe. If you wish, you can add a ham bone or a few pieces of bacon to the Instant Pot and sauté for 5 minutes before commencing the recipe.

Garam Masala Spiced Chickpeas

Indian spices permeate this fragrant dish. Don't let the long ingredient list dissuade you from preparing this recipe; if you don't already have the spices in your pantry, you can find them in the bulk spice bins of most health food stores.

Serves 6 to 8

Prep time: 5 minutes | **Cook time:** 45 minutes | **Release time:** 30 minutes

Jar size: 4 cups

GF | AF | VGN

Dry ingredients

2 tablespoons garam masala

1 teaspoon ground coriander

1 teaspoon paprika

1 teaspoon ground turmeric

1 teaspoon ground cumin

1 teaspoon sea salt

⅓ cup dried onions

1 teaspoon dried garlic

¼ cup sundried tomatoes

3 cups dried chickpeas

For cooking and serving

6 cups vegetable broth or water

Preparation: Layer the dry ingredients in the jar in the order listed.

To Cook: Place all of the jarred ingredients into the Instant Pot. Add 6 cups of vegetable broth or water. Stir to mix. Cover with the lid and ensure the vent is in the "sealed" position. Pressure cook on high for 45 minutes. Allow the steam pressure to release naturally for 30 minutes, then release any remaining pressure manually.

Tip: If the chickpeas are not fully cooked through, return the Instant Pot to simmer to continue cooking.

Curried Lentil Soup

If you think lentil soup is boring, think again! This spicy, savory soup packs a flavor punch from curry powder, plenty of garlic, and a tangy salsa to go on top. If you don't feel like pulling together the salsa ingredients, a squeeze of lemon juice will do the trick. This recipe is adapted from *Vedge*, one of my favorite vegan cookbooks. This soup is easy to begin with, but the Instant Pot makes it a cinch.

Serves 6 to 8

Prep time: 5 minutes | **Cook time:** 15 minutes | **Release time:** 10 minutes

Jar size: 4 cups

GF | AF | VGN

Dry ingredients

2 tablespoons curry powder

½ teaspoon sea salt

1 teaspoon dried garlic

⅓ cup dried onion

3 cups dried green lentils

For cooking and serving

10 cups vegetable broth or water

Preparation: Layer the dry ingredients in the jar in the order listed.

To Cook: Place all of the jarred ingredients into the Instant Pot. Add 10 cups of vegetable broth or water. Stir to mix. Cover with the lid and ensure the vent is in the "sealed" position. Pressure cook on high for 15 minutes. Allow the steam pressure to release naturally for 10 minutes, then release any remaining pressure manually.

Remove about 4 cups of the soup and place them into a blender. Cover the blender with a lid and a towel, but ensure the lid is vented to allow some of the steam to escape. Puree until smooth. Return the pureed lentils to the pot of soup and stir to mix.

Serve with the cilantro and red onion salsa (recipe on page 96).

Cilantro and Red Onion Salsa

½ bunch fresh cilantro

½ red onion, minced

¾ teaspoon sea salt

1 lemon, juice only

Combine all of the ingredients in a small bowl and allow to rest for about 15 to 20 minutes before serving.

Three-Bean Vegan Chili

I have been making some version of this vegan chili for at least a decade since my friend Lynn shared it with me. What really makes it are the mushrooms—their earthy flavor and meaty texture really add another dimension to the chili. Although this recipe has far more ingredients than some of the other recipes in this book, the effect is beautiful in a glass jar and worth the trip to the store to gather each ingredient.

Serves 6

Prep time: 5 minutes | **Cook time:** 40 minutes | **Release time:** 20 minutes
Jar size: 4 cups

GF | AF | VGN

Dry ingredients

2 tablespoons chili powder

1 tablespoon smoked paprika

½ tablespoon ground cumin

1 teaspoon dried garlic

½ teaspoon sea salt

⅓ cup dried onion

2 tablespoons dried celery

2 tablespoons dried carrots

2 tablespoons diced dried mushrooms, such as porcini or shiitake

2 tablespoons sundried tomatoes

½ cup dried black beans

½ cup pinto beans

½ cup great northern or cannellini beans

For cooking and serving

6 cups vegetable broth or water

Preparation: Layer the dry ingredients in the jar in the order listed.

To Cook: Place all of the jarred ingredients into the Instant Pot. Add 6 cups of vegetable broth or water. Stir to mix. Cover with the lid and ensure the vent is in the "sealed" position. Pressure cook on high for 40 minutes. Allow the steam pressure to release naturally for 20 minutes, then release any remaining pressure manually.

Ingredient Tip: The three beans used in this chili cook at roughly the same rate. If you want to swap any of these beans for another, choose one that cooks in roughly the same amount of time, such as navy beans. If you use kidney beans, know that they cook more quickly, in about 15 to 20 minutes, so they may be slightly overdone and falling apart.

Spicy Lentil Taco Filling

This recipe is adapted from one shared by Dana Shultz of the blog and cookbook *Minimalist Baker*. As much as I love her version and make it often, I wanted one that was slightly less time consuming and could be prepared in one dish using dried lentils. I also wanted to be able to share a jar of it with friends and family as a yummy vegan stand-in on taco Tuesdays.

Serves 6

Prep time: 5 minutes | **Cook time:** 15 minutes | **Release time:** 10 minutes

Jar size: 3½ to 4 cups

GF | AF | VGN

Dry ingredients

1 tablespoon ground chipotle

1 tablespoon ground cumin

1 tablespoon smoked paprika

¼ teaspoon ground cloves

2 teaspoons dried oregano

2 tablespoons brown sugar

2 teaspoons sea salt

⅓ cup dried onion

1 teaspoon dried garlic

½ cup dried carrots

2 cups dried lentils

For cooking and serving

4 cups vegetable broth or water

2 tablespoons lime juice, to serve

Preparation: Layer the ingredients in the jar in the order listed.

To Cook: Place all of the dry ingredients into the Instant Pot. Add 4 cups of vegetable broth or water. Stir to mix. Cover with the lid and ensure the vent is in the "sealed" position. Pressure cook on high for 15 minutes. Allow the steam pressure to release naturally for 10 minutes, then release any remaining pressure manually.

To Serve: Stir in 2 tablespoons of freshly squeezed lime juice.

Ingredient Tip: Choose Mexican oregano for a slightly bolder flavor in this recipe.

Cannellini Beans with Chorizo Spice

When I first learned that I could use the spices in chorizo and add them to just about anything to give it that punchy chorizo flavor, I was so thrilled. Of course, if you want to add 8 ounces of actual chorizo to your Instant Pot before cooking this recipe, go for it! Sauté for about 5 to 7 minutes until just cooked through, then add the remaining ingredients.

Serves 6 to 8

Prep time: 5 minutes | **Cook time:** 35 minutes | **Release time:** 20 minutes

Jar size: 3½ to 4 cups

GF | AF | VGN

Dry ingredients

2 cups dried cannellini beans

¼ cup thinly sliced sundried tomatoes

⅓ cup dried onion

1 teaspoon dried garlic

1 tablespoon dried oregano

1 tablespoon smoked paprika

1 teaspoon ground cumin

1 teaspoon ground coriander

⅛ teaspoon ground cloves

2 teaspoons sea salt

2 dried bay leaves

For cooking and serving

6 cups vegetable broth or water

4 cups roughly chopped fresh spinach, to serve

2 teaspoons red wine vinegar, to serve

Preparation: Layer the dry ingredients in the jar in the order listed.

To Cook: Place all of the jarred ingredients into the Instant Pot. Add 6 cups of vegetable broth or water. Stir to mix. Cover with the lid and ensure the vent is in the "sealed" position. Pressure cook on high for 35 minutes. Allow the steam pressure to release naturally for 20 minutes, then release any remaining pressure manually.

To Serve: Stir in 4 cups roughly chopped fresh spinach and 2 teaspoons red wine vinegar.

Ingredient Tip: Choose sundried tomatoes that are not packed in oil.

Dhal

Enjoy this spicy vegan stew with basmati rice and stewed greens, or just top with some fresh cilantro and a squeeze of lime juice.

Serves 8

Prep time: 5 minutes | **Cook time:** 10 minutes | **Release time:** 10 minutes

Jar size: 9 cups

GF | AF | VGN

Dry ingredients

2 teaspoons ground cumin

1 teaspoon ground ginger

1½ teaspoons ground turmeric

1 tablespoon curry powder

½ teaspoon cayenne pepper

1 teaspoon sea salt

½ cup dried onion

1 teaspoon dried garlic

2 tablespoons roughly chopped sun-dried tomatoes

3 cups dried yellow lentils

For cooking and serving

6 cups vegetable broth or water

Preparation: Layer the dry ingredients in the jar in the order listed.

To Cook: Place all of the jarred ingredients into the Instant Pot. Add 6 cups of vegetable broth or water. Stir to mix. Cover with the lid and ensure the vent is in the "sealed" position. Pressure cook on high for 10 minutes. Allow the steam pressure to release naturally for 10 minutes, then release any remaining pressure manually.

Ingredient Tip: Choose sundried tomatoes that are not packed in oil.

Southern Black-Eyed Peas

Smoky bacon, spicy red chile flakes, and savory onion, bell pepper, and celery permeate this delicious Southern favorite. Serve it alongside stewed collard greens and corn bread for a complete meal.

Serves 6 to 8

Prep time: 5 minutes | **Cook time:** 20 minutes | **Release time:** 15 minutes

Jar size: 3½ to 4 cups

GF | **AF**

Dry ingredients

¼ cup real bacon bits

2 tablespoons smoked paprika

¼ teaspoon red chile flakes

⅓ cup dried onion

2 teaspoons dried garlic

¼ cup dried celery

¼ cup dried bell pepper

1 teaspoon dried thyme

1 teaspoon sea salt

2¾ cups dried black-eyed peas

For cooking and serving

6 cups chicken broth or water

1 tablespoon balsamic vinegar, to serve

Preparation: Layer the dry ingredients in the jar in the order listed.

To Cook: Place all of the jarred ingredients into the Instant Pot. Add 6 cups of chicken broth or water. Stir to mix. Cover with the lid and ensure the vent is in the "sealed" position. Pressure cook on high for 20 minutes. Allow the steam pressure to release naturally for 15 minutes, then release any remaining pressure manually.

To Serve: Stir in 1 tablespoon of balsamic vinegar.

Tip: To make this recipe vegan, omit the bacon bits and replace the chicken broth with vegetable broth.

Wild Mushroom and Farro Stew

Whether you hike through rugged forests, surf a chilly winter swell, or spend your day on the ski slopes, this protein-packed soup is a perfect fall and winter dish after a day of adventuring. The Instant Pot makes it easy to make it in the morning and leave it on warm all day for a comforting meal to come home to.

Serves 6 to 8

Prep time: 5 minutes | **Cook time:** 45 minutes | **Release time:** 20 minutes

Jar size: 3½ to 4 cups

GF | **AF**

Dry ingredients

¼ cup dried onion

1 teaspoon dried garlic

1 teaspoon dried thyme

1 teaspoon dried rosemary

½ teaspoon sea salt

½ cup dried assorted mushrooms, such as porcini, shiitake, oyster, and wild mushrooms

1 cup dried chickpeas

1½ cups dried farro

For cooking and serving

10 cups chicken broth

1 teaspoon sherry vinegar or red wine vinegar

Preparation: Layer the dry ingredients in the jar in the order listed.

To Cook: Place all of the jarred ingredients into the Instant Pot. Add 10 cups of chicken broth. Stir to mix. Cover with the lid and ensure the vent is in the "sealed" position. Pressure cook on high for 45 minutes. Allow the steam pressure to release naturally for at least 20 minutes, then release any remaining pressure manually or allow the stew to remain on warm until you're ready to serve.

Kale and White Bean Soup

Kale chips find a new home in this white bean soup with rosemary, thyme, and plenty of hearty garden vegetables. Choose kale that has been dehydrated with minimal other ingredients, ideally just sea salt and perhaps a touch of olive oil. Adjust the seasoning of the soup after cooking—it may need more salt, but that's dependent on how much salt was in the kale chips.

Serves 6

Prep time: 5 minutes | **Cook time:** 45 minutes | **Release time:** 15 minutes
Jar size: 4 cups

GF | AF

Dry ingredients

¼ cup dried onion

¼ cup dried carrots

¼ cup dried celery

1 teaspoon dried rosemary

1 teaspoon dried thyme

¼ cup sundried tomatoes

¼ teaspoon sea salt

2 cups dried cannellini beans

1 cup dried kale

For cooking and serving

10 cups chicken broth or water

Preparation: Layer the dry ingredients in the jar in the order listed.

To Cook: Place all of the ingredients into the Instant Pot. Add 10 cups of chicken broth or water. Stir to mix. Cover with the lid and ensure the vent is in the "sealed" position. Pressure cook on high for 45 minutes. Allow the steam pressure to release naturally for 15 minutes, then release any remaining pressure manually.

Ingredient Tip: Choose sundried tomatoes that are not packed in oil. The kale chips will not remain crunchy when stored in the mason jar with the other ingredients. But this is fine. They'll become soft during cooking anyway.

Ethiopian Red Lentil Soup

My church shares its building with an Ethiopian congregation, which has introduced me to the spice berbere (BER-bur-ay). It's actually a spice blend—like curry powder or garam masala—and is comprised of onion powder, cardamom, coriander, nutmeg, cloves, cinnamon, and allspice. I prefer to purchase my spice blend rather than mixing it myself. The pungent flavors and aromas of the spices permeate the red lentils. Make sure to finish the soup off with the lime juice. The black mustard seeds aren't essential, but they look beautiful in the jar and bring complexity to the otherwise quite simple lentil stew.

Serves 6

Prep time: 5 minutes | **Cook time:** 5 minutes | **Release time:** 10 minutes
Jar size: 3 cups

GF | AF | VGN

Dry ingredients

2 teaspoons berbere

1 teaspoon sea salt

1 teaspoon ground turmeric

2 cups dried red lentils

⅓ cup dried onion

2 tablespoons black mustard seeds

For cooking and serving

9 cups vegetable broth or water

2 tablespoons freshly squeezed lime juice, to serve

Preparation: Layer the dry ingredients in the jar in the order listed.

To Cook: Place all of the jarred ingredients into the Instant Pot. Add 9 cups of vegetable broth or water. Stir to mix. Cover with the lid and ensure the vent is in the "sealed" position. Pressure cook on high for 5 minutes. Allow the steam pressure to release naturally for 10 minutes, then release any remaining pressure manually.

To Serve: Stir in the freshly squeezed lime juice.

Tuscan Minestrone Soup

This soup marries all of the classic minestrone ingredients into a single jar, making it a safe bet for gift giving. Everyone from the adventurous foodie to the older relatives who appreciate tradition will love it!

Serves 6

Prep time: 5 minutes | **Cook time:** 35 minutes | **Release time:** 5 minutes

Jar size: 3½ to 4 cups

GF | **AF** | **VGN**

Dry ingredients

⅓ cup dried onion

2 teaspoons dried garlic

1 tablespoon Italian herb blend

¼ cup dried celery

¼ cup dried carrot

1 teaspoon sea salt

¼ cup thinly sliced sundried tomatoes

1 cup kidney beans

½ cup orzo pasta or pasta shells

¾ cup dried kale chips

For cooking and serving

9 cups vegetable broth or water

2 teaspoons balsamic vinegar, to serve

Preparation: Layer the dry ingredients in the jar in the order listed.

To Cook: Place all of the jarred ingredients into the Instant Pot. Add 9 cups of vegetable broth or water. Stir to mix. Cover with the lid and ensure the vent is in the "sealed" position. Pressure cook on high for 35 minutes. Allow the steam pressure to release naturally for 5 minutes, then release any remaining pressure manually.

To Serve: Stir in the balsamic vinegar.

CHAPTER 7

Desserts & Drinks

Five-Spice Apple Compote

Use this as a filling for apple pie or to ladle over vanilla ice cream. Chinese five-spice powder adds a little spice to the traditional flavors of apple compote. It already contains cinnamon, but my mother-in-law, who taught me to make apple pie, says there's no such thing as too much cinnamon. I tend to agree, so don't skimp!

Serves 4

Prep time: 5 minutes | **Cook time:** 3 minutes | **Release time:** 10 minutes

Jar size: 4 cups

GF | AF | V

Dry ingredients

½ cup brown sugar

1 teaspoon Chinese five-spice powder

2 teaspoons ground cinnamon

¼ teaspoon sea salt

3½ cups dried apples, sliced

For cooking and serving

4 cups apple juice or water

¼ cup butter, cut into pieces

Preparation: Layer the dry ingredients in the jar in the order listed.

To Cook: Place all of the jarred ingredients into the Instant Pot. Add 4 cups of apple juice or water. Stir to mix. Place the butter pieces over the apple mixture. Cover with the lid and ensure the vent is in the "sealed" position. Pressure cook on high for 3 minutes. Allow the steam pressure to release naturally for 10 minutes, then release any remaining pressure manually.

Double Dark Chocolate Cake

Brown sugar adds complexity to this decadent, dark chocolate cake.

Serves 8

Prep time: 5 minutes | **Cook time:** 30 minutes | **Release time:** 10 minutes

Jar size: 4 cups

V

Dry ingredients

1 cup brown sugar

1¾ cups all-purpose flour

1 teaspoon baking soda

½ teaspoon baking powder

¼ cup buttermilk powder

¾ teaspoon sea salt

½ cup unsweetened cocoa powder

½ cup dark chocolate chips

For cooking and serving

2 eggs

½ cup oil

1 cup water or hot coffee

Preparation: Layer the dry ingredients in the jar in the order listed.

To Cook: Place the jarred ingredients into a bowl and add the eggs, oil, and water or coffee. Stir to mix thoroughly until no lumps remain.

Coat the interior of a 6-cup nonstick fluted tube pan, such as a Bundt pan, with cooking spray. Spread the cake batter into the tube pan and cover with aluminum foil.

Add one additional cup of water to the Instant Pot.

If needed, make a sling for the pan using the method described on page 12. Place the trivet in the bottom of the Instant Pot and carefully lower the cake pan onto the trivet. Close the Instant Pot lid and ensure the vent is in the "sealed" position. Pressure cook on high for 30 minutes. Allow the steam pressure to release naturally for 10 minutes, then release any remaining pressure manually.

Carefully remove the tube pan using the sling and allow it to cool for about 15 minutes. Carefully invert the pan onto a plate and allow the cake to cool the rest of the way.

Pineapple Coconut Bread

Enjoy a taste of the tropics in this tasty bread filled with dried pineapple and toasted coconut.

Serves 8

Prep time: 5 minutes | **Cook time:** 35 minutes | **Release time:** 10 minutes

Jar size: 4 cups

V

Dry ingredients

1 cup granulated sugar

1½ cups all-purpose flour

1 teaspoon baking soda

½ teaspoon baking powder

¾ teaspoon sea salt

1 cup finely chopped dried pineapple

½ cup unsweetened, shredded coconut, toasted

For cooking and serving

2 eggs

½ cup oil

¾ cup coconut milk

1 teaspoon vanilla extract

Preparation: Layer the dry ingredients in the jar in the order listed.

To Cook: Place the jarred ingredients into a bowl and add the eggs, oil, coconut milk, and vanilla. Stir to mix thoroughly until no lumps remain.

Coat the interior of a 6-cup nonstick fluted tube pan, such as a Bundt pan, with cooking spray. Spread the cake batter into the tube pan and cover with aluminum foil.

Add 1 additional cup of water to the Instant Pot.

If needed, make a sling for the pan using the method described on page 12. Place the trivet in the bottom of the Instant Pot and carefully lower the cake pan onto the trivet. Close the Instant Pot lid and ensure the vent is in the "sealed" position. Pressure cook on high for 35 minutes. Allow the steam pressure to release naturally for 10 minutes, then release any remaining pressure manually.

Carefully remove the tube pan using the sling and allow it to cool for about 15 minutes. Carefully invert the pan onto a plate and allow the cake to cool the rest of the way.

Vanilla-Scented Rice Pudding

Rice pudding is comfort food and sophistication all in one dish. The subtly sweetened, fragrant vanilla pudding is creamy and rich without being over the top. It's ready in a flash in the Instant Pot, so when you're craving something sweet, you're all set.

Serves 6 to 8

Prep time: 5 minutes | **Cook time:** 8 minutes | **Release time:** 10 minutes
Jar size: 4 cups

GF | **V**

Dry ingredients

¼ teaspoon sea salt

¼ teaspoon cinnamon

¼ cup brown sugar

1 whole vanilla bean, split along one side

3 cups arborio or short-grain white rice

¾ cup raisins

For cooking and serving

4½ cups water

½ cup heavy cream or coconut cream

Preparation: Layer the dry ingredients in the jar in the order listed.

To Cook: Place all of the jarred ingredients into the Instant Pot. Add 4½ cups of water. Stir to mix. Cover with the lid and ensure the vent is in the "sealed" position. Pressure cook on high for 8 minutes. Allow the steam pressure to release naturally for 10 minutes, then release any remaining pressure manually. Stir in the heavy cream or coconut cream and allow to rest for 5 minutes before serving.

Ingredient Tip: To split the vanilla bean, make a small cut down one side of the pod. This will allow all of the insides of the vanilla bean to permeate the pudding. To make this recipe vegan and dairy-free, substitute the heavy cream with coconut cream.

Mulled Wine

Mulled wine sounds easy—just cook wine with sugar, citrus, and a handful of spices—but it's not. Cook for too long, and you lose all of the alcohol. Cook for too little time, and you don't get all of the flavor from the aromatic ingredients. The Instant Pot makes mulled wine in, well, an instant, and it preserves most of the alcohol.

Makes 6 cups

Prep time: 5 minutes | **Cook time:** 1 minute | **Release time:** 0 minutes
Jar size: 1½ to 2 cups

GF | AF | VGN

Dry ingredients

1 cup granulated sugar

2 whole cinnamon sticks

½ cup dehydrated apple slices

5 to 7 whole cloves

3 whole star anise

2 teaspoons dried orange zest

For cooking and serving

2 (750 ml) bottles red wine

Preparation: Layer the dry ingredients in the jar in the order listed.

To Cook: Place all of the jarred ingredients into the Instant Pot. Add the bottles of red wine. Stir to mix. Cover with the lid and ensure the vent is in the "sealed" position. Pressure cook on high for 1 minute. Press cancel and unplug the pressure cooker from the outlet. Use the quick-release function to release the pressure in quick bursts.

Safety Tip: Be careful as you release the pressure from the valve because it contains evaporated alcohol. Make sure there are no open flames nearby and avert your face, as usual, from the vent.

Alternate Method: You can also choose to cook the mulled wine using the slow cook function for 2 hours.

Spiced Chai

My husband spent three weeks in India where chai tea was a daily habit. It was served in very small clay cups that could be discarded on the ground. This version uses all of the traditional spices. Clay cups are optional.

Makes 8 cups

Prep time: 5 minutes | **Cook time:** 1 minute | **Release time:** 5 minutes

Jar size: 1½ to 2 cups

GF | V

Dry ingredients

4 cinnamon sticks

½ cup brown sugar

½ cup loose black tea

3 tablespoons sliced dried ginger

2½ teaspoons black peppercorns

12 cardamom pods

For cooking and serving

8 cups water

½ cup heavy cream

Preparation: Layer the dry ingredients in the jar in the order listed.

To Cook: Place all of the jarred ingredients into the Instant Pot. Add 8 cups of water and heavy cream. Stir to mix. Cover with the lid and ensure the vent is in the "sealed" position. Pressure cook on high for 1 minute. Allow the steam pressure to release naturally for 5 minutes, then release any remaining pressure manually.

To Serve: Carefully pour the liquid through a fine mesh sieve to strain out the solid ingredients. Serve immediately.

Ingredient Tip: If you don't have access to loose tea, simply open the contents of several bags of tea to yield ½ cup.

Resources

Books

Clark, Melissa. *Dinner in an Instant: 75 Modern Recipes for Your Pressure Cooker, Multicooker, and Instant Pot®*. New York: Clarkson Potter, 2017.

Ellgon, Pamela. *The Ultimate Healthy Dehydrator Cookbook. 150 Recipes to Make and Cook with Dehydrated Foods*. Berkeley, CA: Sonoma Press, 2016.

Landau, Rich, and Kate Jacoby. *Vedge: 100 Plates Large and Small That Redefine Vegetable Cooking*. New York: The Experiment, 2015.

Lawson, Nigella. *How to Be a Domestic Goddess: Baking and the Art of Comfort Cooking*. New York: Hachette Books, 2002.

Martin, Roberto, and Quentin Bacon. *Vegan Cooking for Carnivores: Over 125 Recipes So Tasty You Wont Miss the Meat*. New York: Hachette Book Group, 2013.

Schieving, Barbara, Chef AJ, Jill Nussinow, et al. *Instant Pot Recipe Booklet, 4th Edition*. Instant Pot Company, 2018.

Websites

Healthy Seasonal Recipes, Gluten Free Walnut and Kale Quinoa Stuffing, www.healthyseasonalrecipes.com/gluten-free-walnut-and-kale-quinoa-stuffing

Hip Pressure Cooking, www.hippressurecooking.com

Instant Pot Eats: How to Cook Different Grains, https://instantpoteats.com/instant-pot-101-how-to-cook-different-grains

Minimalist Baker: 1-Pot Vegan "Barbacoa," https://minimalistbaker.com/1-pot-vegan-barbacoa

Conversions

Volume

U.S.	U.S. EQUIVALENT	METRIC
1 tablespoon (3 teaspoons)	½ fluid ounce	15 milliliters
¼ cup	2 fluid ounces	60 milliliters
⅓ cup	3 fluid ounces	90 milliliters
½ cup	4 fluid ounces	120 milliliters
⅔ cup	5 fluid ounces	150 milliliters
¾ cup	6 fluid ounces	180 milliliters
1 cup	8 fluid ounces	240 milliliters
2 cups	16 fluid ounces	480 milliliters

Weight

U.S.	METRIC
½ ounce	15 grams
1 ounce	30 grams
2 ounces	60 grams
¼ pound	115 grams
⅓ pound	150 grams
½ pound	225 grams
¾ pound	350 grams
1 pound	450 grams

Temperature

FAHRENHEIT (°F)	CELSIUS (°C)
70°F	20°C
100°F	40°C
120°F	50°C
130°F	55°C
140°F	60°C
150°F	65°C
160°F	70°C
170°F	75°C
180°F	80°C
190°F	90°C
200°F	95°C
220°F	105°C
240°F	115°C
260°F	125°C
280°F	140°C
300°F	150°C
325°F	165°C
350°F	175°C
375°F	190°C
400°F	200°C
425°F	220°C
450°F	230°C

About the Author

Pamela Ellgen is a food blogger at Surfgirleats.com and cookbook author of *Mastering Meal Prep, Sheet Pan Ketogenic, Cast Iron Paleo*, and *Soup & Comfort*. Her work has been featured in *Outside Magazine*, TODAY food, Healthline, *Huffington Post, Edible Phoenix*, and *The Portland Tribune*. When she's not in the kitchen, Pamela enjoys surfing, practicing yoga, and playing with her kids. She lives in California with her husband and two children.